WHAT HAPPENED AT DINNER,
AND AFTER

What Happened at Dinner, and After

poems
by

Warren Cooper

Published by:
BLAST PRESS
324B Matawan Avenue
Cliffwood, NJ 07721
(732) 970-8409
gregglory@aol.com
gregglory.com/blastpress

Contents

The work of words — a poet's psalm 9

Black River
Black River 13
Trapper 16
Another fall 18
Bird with a broken wing 20
The book signing (a short confession) 21
Ghost 22
In the kitchen, naked 23
Every spring, lately 25
A prayer for the dead 27
Fragile things 29

Always ask objective questions
Stunning feats of laundry 33
Always ask objective questions 35
Feeble Gravity 37
Full moon five nights —What his father told him about his birth 40
Max starts eighth grade 42
For Daniel 44
My Great Uncle Max 46
Old Man Spencer loved his chickens 47
Windup watch 49

Frenchtown
Break Neck Life 53
In praise of mosquitoes 54
Fourth of July, 2014 55

Halloween trick or treat, 2010 57
I am the dew 59
This morning 60
Ode to Frenchtown, or, Why I live here 61

Lost herd of horses
To Gail Cross, captain of our high school cheerleading squad 65
I hated him 67
Lost herd of horses 73
Many places 75
Roosevelt dime 76
Six poems about crows, by one who loves them 78
Deli Man 82
Starlings 84

Of love
What happened at dinner, and after 89
Of love 91
What is there to talk about? (after reading Rilke on Rodin) 93
We fall asleep loving and wake together laughing 94
From the earth to the moon, and back 97
James Beard was a great bedtime reader of cookbooks 99
Shadow in the dark 100
Sunrise 102
At last, the gift 104

For Bonnie

The work of words

Lord, teach me the language of everyday work.
Help me to learn the names of tools in the grip of work
the watchmaker's loupe, balance pivot, escape pinion
the smith's ballpeen, anvil, clink.

Teach me, too, the cost of work,
the glassblower's callused palms,
burns on the backs of the grill man's hands,
the cabinetmaker's scarred fingers fitting a joint,
the chemist with blackened nails etched by acid.

Let me hear birdsong fall about the work, shaping it.

Help me understand that we grow by shedding skin,
leaving us at our most vulnerable
when we most need toughness,
how in the dizzying whirl of sun and black sky,
language as plain as water-and-aspirin can support the shaken.

Help me remember that everywhere and always,
words build up and grind away, prop scenery,
fill emptiness, discover frontiers, reclaim the forgotten,
give voice to sweat and muscle, to blood and bruise.

Oh Lord, in this endless desert day, lead me
along a silken river of shimmering moonlight
to an oasis, from fig tree to fig tree,
to where words cling heavily on a narrow branch
fragrant, swollen, waiting to be plucked,
nectar, blood, marrow pooling at the tips of
purposed fingers to rough a map of the true journey.

Black River

Black River

Today, under an inch of snow
and six inches of ice, the
Black River breaches its banks.
pools beneath our bed and
grabs your ankles, howling.

"It's bad," you say, going under.
"More war." We cling to each other,
mortise and tenon.

While you sleep, the Black River
does Jews' work, heaving great
blocks of black ice one atop the
next until your fever melts every-
thing, leaving a pyramid crumbling
in the desert.

Today your voice is that of
stiffly curled oak leaves that
cling to twisted twigs and branches
and hiss in late December gusts.
Behind your eyes a mudslide rakes
away another Lenape village that had clung
to the riverbank by its teeth and
eyebrows for five thousand years.

Today, you scold me about the
government through clenched teeth.
When you say, "Men in suits hide
behind the lady in the harbor,"
I nod in agreement. "They're lice,"

you hiss, "no pickier about dinner
than vultures."

Then I hold you close as you dance
away into the vast everything.
"Tighter," you whisper. "Let me go."
Then you sleep again.

Later you will drop the peppermill
and exhaust yourself chasing
peppercorns across the granite countertop.
When spilt milk soaks the
cookbook you've built over a
lifetime I think that you will
certainly cry, but you laugh, ashen.
"How about this one for dinner,"
you say, pointing to where the
white flood has carried off the ink
and left in its wake a blank page.
You jab and say,
"It's a recipe for disaster."

When you sleep again I try to
peel apart the pages that instead
come away in clumps
as had your hair.

Today, the last day, we're holding
hands in a sunny spot on the
snow-covered deck, wrapped
against the cold in layers, like
mummies. You've grown so small
that our twined fingers find room
in a single mitten.

Suddenly, you're a shy child. "When I die," you say, "will you come with me?" I say, "Yes."

Trapper

I never told you
of the fox that
trotted carefully across the open field
only to step where I knew it must
near the tumbled wall at the edge of the wood
then without knowing, its eyes on more distant things,
walked blindly, black nose, eyes and ears,
into my looped wire noose.

I never told you that
the red fox, tethered by steel wire
to the driven pin, ran all night in a circle,
wearing a path to nowhere
beside the tumbled wall
at the edge of the field of mustard
mostly buried beneath six inches of snow.
The red fox with black feet
and a black snout, panting in the morning moonlight
eyeing me with a narrow, hot look,
foam on its chops, twitching its brush
as far from me as the wire would allow.

I never told you
that I swung an ax handle silken with use
to crush the skull of the fox
smashing it between its hot black eyes,
that it died without a shudder, just
dropped as would a bludgeoned
horse or beeve at slaughter.

I never told you that

the moon was low behind us
me and the red fox that I carried, with its
black snout and feet,
that the sun paused briefly below the horizon
our single long shadow was
stippled by spines of mustard poking through the snow,
that the dead fox had a white patch at the tip of his tail,
that his pink tongue lolled as I gripped his throat in my left hand,
my right hand holding the ax handle,
that his velvet ears pointed stiffly, as though still listening
and that I blocked his body, with its unsheathed glistening pink
    penis
from the view of the woman jogging along the road,
her red hair tied back in a swinging ponytail.

I never told you that
that her far-cast eyes
were on the coming dawn
and she never noticed me
or the fox or the handle of the ax.

I never told you these things.

I never told you anything.

Another fall

The mulberry trees near the fence
hunch over the lawn and the pasture
shaking in the shuddering wind
like shaggy dogs vomiting after eating grass.
They shed water from their wet-dogs' coats
and huddle like the horses do, standing in the field below,
shaking their heads and blowing rain from their lips
their heavy haunches streaming darkly with rainwater
turning from time to time to look over their withers
at the tossing branches, at everything moving
at everything that in my eyes is harbinger of wild winter.

The dark sky presses inside
as it does on wet fall mornings
and I turn on the kitchen light to make breakfast
or at least to make noise with pots and pans.
Through the rain-rippled glass I see
maple leaves and oak leaves and nuts from shagbark hickories
trapped among the knots of the rope-weave hammock
strung between two small black chestnut-trees.
Just days before, mowing the lawn shirtless and barefoot,
I set a folding chair on that sun-bleached hammock and now,
with its metal arms spread, it clings
to the cargo-netting rocking in the wind like
a sick sailor hot-sheeted among hundreds
in the hull of a heaving Navy ship headed out to war.

I don't know what I want
for this first real fall breakfast —
if not the heat of summer
and the bright light of an August morning

bounding off the porch and bursting the screen
of an open window like a too-eager hound.
But I do know that I still want sweet fruit, not citrus,
nothing more tart than an under-ripe strawberry.
I want pulpy melon, chin-drooling peaches and
juice-spurting plums with flesh the color of a woman's sex,
fruit that doesn't need to be chewed to eat.
I don't want steaming oatmeal yet
or hot farina shimmering with jeweled flecks of butter.
I don't want to be wondering, as I do now,
my bare feet numb with cold, where my damn socks are.
I don't want to desire comfort food yet,
the hot spread of sunshine is still condiment enough.

Raindrops clatter at the kitchen window like pebbles
thrown by a determined, loathed suitor,
and the waterlogged heads of goldenrod bob and nod
waiting alas for a last benediction of sun.
Ragged chevrons of Canada geese arch south
through cloud-clotted skies, and I recall Monday's
migrations of goldfinches, of cardinals, of orioles, bluebirds
and red-breasted robins I know I'll never see again.

In the long gray dawn of early autumn
with help from the first cold rainfall
the wind tears loose yellow and orange and red leaves
and even some that are still heavy and green
and sends them from the trees into the active air
then to the sodden ground one after another
like wet facecloths dropped on pavement.
As they lay there, like trash tossed from a carful of teenagers,
I congratulate myself again, for being smart enough,
unlike Hemingway, to not own a shotgun.

Bird with a broken wing

At summer's end when
the rain came and came
and the car failed and food spoiled and
papers piled high on the broken chair
spilled from the porch to
blow across the neglected lawn,
the last thing you said
letting the screen door slam
and heading down the lane
was something about trash
I didn't quite catch
studying, as I was, a feral cat
stalk a bird with a broken wing
beneath the blueberry bush.

The book signing
(a short confession)

Suddenly I'm again an old bird dog trolling the edge of a field,
tongue lolling, taken by an insistent scent
along a path I hadn't traveled since we met,
yet as familiar as a package with the label turned away.

The hairs of my neck stiffen,
ears twitch forward and back,
my mouth fills then dries,
hot breath scrapes my tongue.

Musical laughter cast from across the room
is a wire snare hidden under fallen leaves. It should
hasten me toward the door, but draws instead.

"O," she says, "I've heard of you."

Her eyes on mine are some color.
Her hair is loose or tied.
The music of her voice presses its palm against my chest.
Her weighted gaze, a trick of light from within,
curls like a beckoning finger of cigarette smoke.

"You're that poet
who writes about
true love," she says,
and her lips part
in a humid smile
of predatory teeth.

Ghost

"Looks it not like the king? Mark it, Horatio." (Shakespeare, Hamlet)

Whose are these gray hairs in the sink?
Whose loose bag of skin between whose trembling thighs?
Teeth in a bedside glass, whose are they?

That's me navigating a bike through
humped trash and tumbled cinderblock
scattered about a seething Newark lot.
That's me clutching the pigskin in the school end zone.
That's me making love the first time
on a park slide in Millburn.

Me signing payroll checks.
Me walking the boardwalk
with one child sleeping in my arms
while the older bets a roulette wheel quarter on MOM.
Me holding my own on a hike
across Hunterdon with 20-year-olds,
window blinds rattling somewhere behind me.

This persistent hiss in this ear, whose is it?
Whose eyes, so sharp they could see beyond distance
and bring the near even closer,
now need these compound lenses?
The spotted and paper-thin skin
on the backs of these hands,
whose is that?

Whose history is this that spreads
like an ink stain on silk,
noisy and wet, already drying?

In the kitchen, naked

It's not as dangerous as you might think
To cook naked, not as dangerous,
For example, as making love on a motorcycle.

You do need good knife skills
And the good sense to handle hot oil carefully,
But mostly it's about forgetting you're naked.

It's probably best not to bake naked, though
The blast of heat from an open oven door
Is murder, as anyone will tell you

Chopping is safe — if you consider your nakedness
And back away from a falling knife rather than try to catch it,
Always a good rule, naked or not.

What gets dicey, naked,
Is handling hot pans and pots of boiling liquids,
Moving scalded vegetables to an ice bath, for example

Use a cloth rather than your bare hand to grab hot handles
Which should point outward, is my advice
At least, naked, no cuffs can catch a handle and scatter things wildly

Still, there will be flares, spills, splashes, spattering of hot oil
(If you keep kosher then bacon is no worry)
And first-timers might consider an apron

I could show you scars — on backs of my hands, and elsewhere —
That would curl your hair, and you have to take care
With chili peppers and garlic and some curries.

It's best to not cook naked when entertaining
At least, not after the guests have arrived
Unless, of course, it's that kind of party

Even so, guests, I find, can be a distraction
When naked in the kitchen,
Though I suppose that's true in any room.

Every spring, lately

When garden tulips and daffodils give way to mountain pink
and muddy purple phlox appears at the edge of the wood,
the lawn becomes a carpet of Johnny jump-ups,
a micro meadow of violets creeps under the shadow of budding
    laurel
and the sisters come again to tie back their wild hair with willow
and stretch slender arms to draw me from my chair,
to skip-step dance through the apple orchard,
their backsides bare beneath billowing gossamer,
to the hidden pond where Faith brings a hand to my shoulder
and Grace sets a palm on my hip and both twine their hands in mine
    in a true love knot,
and Charity turns in place to music as faint as a loosed feather.

Humming the earth's deep hum, our noses filled with spring grass,
our breath filled with youthsong and sweet lilac,
under the sun, under the moon
under the sweep of uncomplicated clouds reflected in pondmirror,
    lilting larksong, hawksong,
we hear a hidden redwing blackbird keening among reeds as thin
    and stiff as porcupine quills
and, naked and beautiful, we slip into the black water
as soundlessly as a canoe parting pondskin.

Then comes a gentle squall of rain drifting so very slowly
as to come nearly unnoticed, dappling and streaming and cooling
settling on our cheeks and hair, on the glowing skin of their breasts
    and thighs,
leaving marks on the backs of my hands, as it always does, in spring,
    lately,
and I'm startled awake to find I've fallen asleep again in my chair

under the first shower of apple blossom petals
and all around me the new grass, reaching and breathless,
sends up the waiting earth's irresistible stink.

A prayer for the dead

You will call, when it comes,
the most accomplished builder of boxes
square and joined
a singular home
for a household of one
a quiet place and still
a grove, a pine hammock hung
between the roots of beeches, black walnuts
everything in quiet repose
everything except lively death.

It must be sealed tightly
fitted together with dove tails
with glistening screws and streaming tears
with clenched fists, solid bolts, wrenched hearts
edges mitered and as certain and as grim as mathematics
as if, were we able to build it perfectly,
it could keep out this salt cure, death.

What is inside is inside no longer
it cannot be housed or even contained
instead, they come to us then
in dreams, in memory, in visions
in random happy accidents of thought
and in hollow, thick-throated moments
of misery, eyes filling, empty-hearted.

Because we can neither keep from them
what has come to them
nor keep from ourselves what is to come,
close the lid loosely

there is, finally, nothing to keep out
nothing sacred to keep hidden inside
outside and inside are the same for all that
and we are all the same, to death.

So let it come, let it come down
without heat, without light
without roar or rage or question
let it come down, this death.

And let us say, Amen.

Fragile things

The discs of the tiller tore the earth every spring,
humping it in long wavering furrows
that smelled wormy and rank and alive.
The dogs would gulp dark dense clumps of it
and find particular places
to drop their shoulders and
squirm around on their backs
then skulk home to be scolded and shunned.
But I envied them their special knowing
and uncontrollable lust.

Once, the big machine turned up fresh guts
bagged in deerhide and they fought over it,
snarling and lunging until he startled them
with a blast from the shotgun he always
carried in those days. Another time he used
a Luger smuggled home after the war to kill
one of them that began drooling, shaking its
head and snapping its teeth at the empty air.

Breakfast was short but dinner was endless.
Lunch was eaten from a box in the tree stand
in an old black walnut thick with bees where
he would prop himself up for hours in winter
with coffee and whisky and slaughter deer
we butchered and packed into a chest in the barn.

I went to school or didn't. He didn't care and
I finally stopped. He spoke when he had something
to say, as often to the tractor as to me
and grew gray and even more quiet until

one spring dawn he suddenly became redfaced
and rigid, staring without seeing then dropped past
the high wheel without warning into a shadowy furrow
that had a particular smell, ready and alive with worms.

Always ask objective questions

Stunning feats of laundry

I'm in the basement doing laundry, thinking,
There's more to inner space than I once thought.
There's space between fabric fibers and space inside the fibers
there's negative space in your patterned skirt, grin-through in
    stretch pants,
in dotted Swiss, in Argyle socks.

In the rock and throb of the big machine, shirts link arms
and sway like kindergarteners singing in a circle
as agitation floods the fabrics' inner spaces.

Lights flicker as the cycle shifts with a thud from wash to rinse to
    spin
and upstairs you're rinsing dishes or rinsing your hair
or spinning in place, dangerously dancing with the universe
moving one narrow foot in dark circles round the other.

When you call me to dinner
I'm stooped under the low ceiling shuffling sideways between
    dripping sheets.
Warm air groans inside the ducts, damp air settles lint in clots.
Our girl has tossed clothes that no longer fit to the crickets in the
    corner
split knees of our boy's jeans grin from a jumbled pile, their frayed
    mouths yawning.

Without warning my great good fortune tightens around me until I
    can hardly breathe.
I recall our first embrace, how I felt at once heavy and weightless to
    near bursting
all the empty space inside me taken up,
the way whipped cream grows both bulky and light,
the way a Ferris wheel fills itself
with its own rising and falling in a spinning circle.

Then I'm suddenly expanding again,
unsteady, ephemeral, swinging up through
the space between us, into the kitchen,
where you stand, one hand on your hip
a wooden spoon to your lips, testing the soup for salt
and I bring you into my arms and in a single breath
conquer the last small space between us.

Always ask objective questions

For my mother

"Siempre faca peruntas objectivas." — Paulo Coelho

Because, with your head covered
    with your wrinkle-lidded eyes closed
    with your slender ringed fingers spread
    you drew circles over the Shabbos candles
and, because you muttered, no
    you mumbled words that might have been
    any language — or no language at all...

And, because baking and not cooking was your joy
    mystical transformation was your life work
    dinner was of little concern
    but dessert was everything
and, because while not unknown to you,
    laughter was not familiar either, nor were rules
    nor even, truth be known, were friends...

Because, the notion of mother
    was either foreign to you or burdensome
    neither objectively nor immediately valuable, you might have said
and, because you preferred to conceal than reveal
    what you truly thought anyway...

And, because your idea of love, if you had one,
    was some inexpressible demon
    demanding, insufferable, ultimately bound up
    or, anyway, transfigured by denial
and, because, anyway, it was you
    who kept us spinning wildly,
    if not crazily, through this singing world...

Because we were always flying off
>even while falling back, turning,
>as if pulled by one elemental force and
>thrust against by another of equal strength
and, because you bound us together by pushing us away
>and insisted that we love one another or risk rough treatment...

And, and, and, because a child bleeds,
>because snow melts, because one must eat to live
>for all these reasons and all other reasons
>I was, at the time, unable to fathom your death
and, because, time turns itself inside out for memory's sake
>all these years later, I still can't.

Feeble Gravity

1
Remember when you were jailed for gambling
    and your most sober son made bail with a rough gesture
Long before that, your wife,
    your first wife, threw herself from a window
    as she said she would, as you said she would
When the tri-fecta paid six thousand dollars
and then the goddam horse died.
The time Clara's cat tore the curtains your second wife had made
And the time you set the couch afire with a smoldering cigar
    while you drunkenly caressed her sister.
The time they found you were just fourteen
    and threw you out of the Merchant Marines.
The time you bought bootleg whiskey for Sinatra
    and ran numbers for Longy Zwillman.
The time you cheated on your third wife
    and all the times she cheated on you.

2
A Cuban cigar, a bay horse at Belmont racing through blowing snow
A tall woman, a glass of warm whiskey when ice was scarce
New shoes that never fit, and a gray felt hat that fit only after you
    grew bald
Children who spoke too fast and friends who suddenly spoke too
    loud
The time you crashed the Studebaker, and before that, the Ford
And before that, overturned
a truckload of Seagram's 7-Crown in Newark
and woke, nine days later,
with a steel plate pressing apart the bones of your skull,
and you pretended not to recognize your fourth wife,
or your third wife, or your children
but knew the bookie who owed you six thousand dollars.

3

Now early sunlight glazes mist that clings to nearby headstones.
Back then it was rosemary russet potatoes, Oysterette crackers,
    black and blue steaks that hung over the plate in Newark Down-the-Port restaurants
    and bled onto white tablecloths your company cleaned for the Portuguese
You slip the paper ring from a Churchill cigar over your granddaughter's thumb
    as she dances to music you can no longer hear
Smoke drifting everywhere
Heavy smoke hanging in layers as still as this mist draped over the dulled bronze grave markers
where pebbles and small stones of remembrance are set along the edges
    felicity, fidelity, perfidy.

4

You put on the salve, you peel an orange, you swallow a worthless pill
Then feeble gravity grows weaker
    another grave empties of its fresh weak light
    and is filled with sudden or foreseen death
And we linger or we scurry or we drift to the edge of the hole
    and peer into it, or try not to peer into it
    and study, instead, the horizon
And meanwhile endure the onslaught of memories
    the way islanders yield to wild weather.

5

We shovel the clotted dirt from a mound
    piled so high for so shallow a hole
Sticky earth clings then falls from the spade

passed hand to hand, striking the thud...thud...thud... pine
muffling distorted voices like white noise
freezing stricken features and softening rough gestures
gestures we'll remember though they were never made.

Full moon five nights —
What his father told him
about his birth

For my 12th grade Drama Teacher, Victor Luca Del Negro.

The first full moon was like hundreds before
sailing on its own light through cloud surf
peeling dark from the bleached bedroom
as your mother's water broke and your elder brother
was born and my father's car wouldn't start and stars
fell like hail on the windshield.

The second full moon the next day birthed your sister,
its busy weight settling like soda ash
where floor meets wall meets ceiling and,
like a rushing flood, brought with it
the AWOL American we found in the basement
who refused to return to his battalion.

A night later the full moon crashed again through the skylight,
and dragged itself by its nails across the room
board by board, leaving a shimmering trail
before flinging itself from the far window
through the morning glory vines to disappear into seared daylight
as daughter two was born with less wit but more wisdom.

On the fourth night of the full moon, we
thought we were ready, when it lifted the lid
of the candy dish to scoop your mother's glittering jewelry
and scurry like a sneak thief down the drain spout,

getting tangled in ivy and barked at by the dog, as your third
sister sucked her first breath and squeezed her fist into my palm.

You were born the fifth night of the full moon
in a true orgasm of heaving and thrusting as that silver globe-fruit
    wobbled
along the tiles of the roof, fell through the skylight and shattered
    glass in tiny shards
across our bed, across your mother's uncrowded belly and became
the sparkling scales on your back and fins that we six clung to
on our wild ride to America through a black and starless night.

Max starts eighth grade

His twitching legs wake him
the morning of the first day of school
before dawn, listening for the sound of the school bus
listening for the sound of juice being poured in the kitchen
for his father's heavy footstep and hesitant knock
the knob already turning in his left hand
meanwhile
The breeze taps the pull of the shade against the open window
two crows rake the quiet morning with their noise
a wedge of Canada geese wheel over the uncut cornfield
and bank sharply, heading vaguely toward Texas
their own racket drowning that of the local crows
and setting off, in the distance, a big dog's deep bark
meanwhile
Sunlight worms to the edge of the window then
comes between the pale shade and the glowing jamb
and angles like a laser along the wall
splinters in the mirror above the cluttered dresser
casts a prism rainbow across the creaking plank floorboards
and across the soft topography of bunched bedding
meanwhile
The shampoo scent of his father's early shower
creeps under the door in eddies
and dust motes ease through the slice of light
and shimmer a moment, and then are gone
meanwhile
A garbage truck grinds gears and comes to a wheezing stop
galvanized cans crash as the trash is tossed inside
one of the men whistles "Crazy" and clings lazily
as the truck heaves and halts along the unpaved country road
and meanwhile

He listens with his eyes closed to all the other sounds
listens through the whirring of insects
and beyond the tock of the clock in the hall.
This is a moment, he thinks, a small moment.
He thinks, I am awake and my legs are twitching to begin.

For Daniel

On the occasion of an insignificant birthday during his middle years

Alas, poor Caliban, you believe you can know
whether you have aged caged or free
because you think freedom is the ability
to act randomly at will.

Where are the dreams you dreamt of freedom in boyhood?
when a bicycle ride whipped tears from your eyes,
when you wore a frayed shirt day after day by choice,
when, Adam, you named every feeling,
every feeling being new to you, you being new to mankind.

Now you wear glasses and
incline your head toward the speaker and
hold steady on the handrail and
come to a full stop —
not knowing if you are truly stopped
or simply waiting to begin again.

Night clouds cradle a waning winter moon
in a sky empty of everything but unreasonable hope
and the scent of wood smoke
which you no longer can truly smell
but only remember.

Thixotropic time slows even as you urge forward, boyo,
compressing this very nanosecond
into the actual moment of becoming.

You effervesce and shed cells,
lose hair, lose teeth, lose opportunity,

and yet, at the actual moment of becoming,
everything worth having is already yours.

My Great Uncle Max

My Uncle Max, a man of many talents
and great sobriety when old
bore three daughters and, like Lear,
learned in age that two had never loved him
lived to see them set out
along sinistral paths that curved inward
as does the shell of the lightning whelk,
so, that when he sought them again in his later years
it was as though he put a chambered shell to his ear
and heard the distance whisper of the sea.

It was his youngest daughter, the last,
clown and wise child
collector of fallen wings and angled surfaces
who, like him, had run wild in her younger days
shedding trinkets to make way
for chance and the unexpected.

It was her murmur, like that of nestlings,
that spoke to the cowl-shrugged man
with his tall stoop, welling with wear,
and with one bright eye glimmering.
It was she who breathed the last comfort
my uncle would hear in this noisy life.
"Papa," she told him. "Rest."

Old Man Spencer loved his chickens

Old Man Spencer said he loved his chickens
more than he loved his children.

First, he'd say, chickens don't live so long.
And when they stopped being productive
you could just eat 'em.

He liked watching them scratch about the yard
and in the stall they shared with an old
deaf and blind mare he could not part with,
bobbing their heads and twitching, using that
queer cooing language he'd come to understand
over the years, to talk their simple talk.

Not like his children, who'd grown vocabularies
beyond what was useful but then
used the same few words over and again,
whether they were useful or otherwise.

Spencer always had more eggs than he could use
but refused to sell them. Instead, he'd store them
in an ancient Kelvinator with a broken handle
he'd wired to the lights in the barn
and kept closed with harness leather.
Only ran when the lights were on,
but it kept the eggs from spoiling.

Once a week he'd walk to a neighbor's house,
as likely ours as another,
and give away what he couldn't eat.

Spencer would say that his chickens
didn't exactly share their food,
but they rarely fought one another bloody
over nonsense, unlike his children.

Like the time the older broke the younger's arm
for teasing about a girlfriend, or
the time the younger set the older's bed afire
because he hadn't repaid on time five dollars she'd lent him.

Chickens came and went, grew, laid,
died, got eaten, got replaced.
Spencer's children, he'd say,
came along one day and never
seemed to go, or when they did,
seemed to come back
with no intention of ever going again.

A day came when the children did leave,
of course, they weren't children anymore.
By then they were too big to eat,
Spencer would say to their mother,
and too tough anyway.

"You wait, Roland," she'd say to him then.
"They'll be back with their own chicks."

And when they did come back,
Spencer's children, with chicks of their own,
Spencer grew mighty fond of them, too.

Windup watch

The concept of time has become
so troublesome for modern science that
determined physicists have decided to simply
do without it, setting the tick tock here now and gone
of life to one side in order to better
explain the constant conversation held between
space and matter in our ten dimensional
universe, which it should be noted,
appears to be slowing down now,
intent, one might say, on stopping
before, we're told, rewinding
in a kind of backward ramble toward the
beginning, which they — most of them, anyway
still call the Big Bang
after which there was a period of time
they have somehow discovered
when time actually accelerated can you imagine rather
than ticking along at its current stolid pace
a pace which, whether measured by the atomic clock
or my grandfather's wristwatch
or the nanosecond counter of your soccer
mom's computer seems unfazed by the
quibbling among famous scientists
who have irrefutably proven —in the lab anyway —
that it (time) will actually stop
at some point, like an old fashioned watch left on the nightstand
while the owner lies in bed with the flu, negligently
allowing it to wind down, having no need
to wear it today — less, actually to even think about time
since going to work is out of the question
and the entire focus of the known universe has narrowed

to a bowl of chicken broth, a slice of toast
and later, whatever that means, a cup of tea
which will sit beside the unwound watch while
the patient sweats out his fever and dreams
awkward, remarkable dreams that feature friends
and events from his childhood and seem so immediate and real
glimpses of which he may remember hours or days from now
when, getting unsteadily ready for the office
he will expand the gold-plated band of the real gold watch
and, as he always does before slipping it over
his hand and into place on his wrist, read the
inscription on the back: To Max, Love Bertha, 1943.

Frenchtown

Break Neck Life

When it is cold like this in spring
    and the moon has set
    black night spreads in all directions like syrup.
Stars glint at every distance
    and a thick mist coils along the Delaware.
There are rare sounds: an owl's pulsing question
    Mr. Passer's cow coughing unseen in the field below the barn
    the furnace trembling, shutting down
    and later, cycling on with a rush.
But mostly quiet and the echo of quiet is embraced here
    quiet that elsewhere clings uneasily to asphalt
    or bleeds onto concrete.
Here, when it is cold like this in spring, and the moon has set
    shadows are indistinguishable from substance
    no light is brighter than that cast by faceted stars centuries ago
When the loudest sound was a thunderclap
    and speed was measured in cords of wood a day
    and strength stood for endurance
    and falling in love took a lifetime.

In praise of mosquitoes

Outside, rain angles into the lawn like tines of a pitch fork
flips pebbles on the pavement
pokes finger-deep holes into the lake.
Inside, a gray moth the size of a golf ball
thuds clumsily again and again against the light fixture.
You, falling through dreams of Indian gods
creating and destroying the universe,
pin me to the mattress with knee, thigh, breast, forearm.
Your hair is against my cheek, your breath on my chest.
Mosquito whine keeps me awake for a while
and I realize how lucky we are that wakefulness
and sleep alternate, that at any minute, you may
open your eyes and turn your lips toward mine
and I will be awake with eyes open to kiss them.

Fourth of July, 2014

We slept late and had to hustle to get to the gym before noon
to peddle miles in place and move weights here and there.
Then George's be-muscled nod and "adios"
saw us off to the Wine Hut for organic Prosecco
then to folding chairs on Kandy and Laine's porch
eating crabs and ribs as the wind pushed sheets of rain
hither and thither, the same wind that wrapped
the Frenchtown Elementary School flag around itself
near the Doughboy statue with its raised fist clutching a grenade
and blew Harry's plastic Uncle Sam top hat into the pool.
As the mayor snored beer-ily in the pocket of his canvas chair,
we raised a glass to our country and wished good will upon its
    citizenry and government
Happy birthday, America. Happy birthday to you.

Our hosts came among us then barefoot and bikinied to refill beer
    cups
and we cheered the children's rainy ballgame
as they giggling slid gamely into muddy home base.
When the fireflies rose from shrubs and lawn we gathered our
    glasses
to walk Indian file through the tree-tunneled dark
along the railway bed turned bike path
to the Delaware River and its steel truss bridge
where we cheered with tipsy oohs and ahhs Doctor Boom's
    fireworks.
Then we kissed one another good night in black-shadowed moonlight
peeling off in pairs and treys to our homes, with complaining
    toddlers at arms
to face two more days of weekend gardening, leftovers, yoga and
    church,

far from war and passion, as far from the constitution as modernity allows.

Happy birthday, America. Happy birthday to you.

Halloween trick or treat, 2010

I'm alone on Bridge Street
at 4 a.m. this wild night with
wind crashing about in waves as harsh
as the howling scent of road kill skunk.
Under the wind's gouging nails, leafless branches
jerk this way and that, the way a heroine
struggles to avoid a loathed suitor's kiss.

I hear the flag's bright hardware clattering
against the bridge keeper's house a block away
while the hissing river below, as black and as
determined as death, pushes toward Trenton.

Piked to the sidewalk, the fourth graders'
papier maché goblins slump
like Christian corpses at the gates of Rome,
glaring at their blind reflections in
shadow-dark shop windows.
Zombies lurch against wind
that shreds their paper skin.
Cracked and crenulated limbs tear free and
fly across the pavement or swing like stumps of crash victims.
The lost left hand of a garish clown still gripping
a rubber axe dripping with red paint blood
bangs madly against the Launderette door.
Scales of a silver dragon sidewalked on its broad belly
outside Schiable's barber shop skitter across
Race Street to press in leafy piles against
dark buildings that lean like headstones.
A lone fairy queen, her yellow mop dreadlocks
snapping about her head like Medusa's snakes,

stretches pencil-thin fingers of one hand
toward its scarlet-nailed mate, lying
in the gutter, gusts lifting and twitching
her golden wand in an ineffective spell.

In a few hours, freed of their lessons,
ballerinas, superheroes, princesses and skeletal ghosts
will parade from the school down Harrison Street
to the bridge keeper's house
where they may as well throw themselves
into the foaming river for all the good that grammar
and geography will do decades from now,
when a sudden wind tears at the lids of their eyes
and like all of us late and soon, they find themselves
sailing alone into death, the bitter end of childhood.

I am the dew

I am the dew that gathers before dawn
on the furred tip of a single blade of grass
among the millions of dewdrops across
the low meadow of lawn beneath your bedroom

I am not a beautiful image of dew
captured in light and midwife'd by
a breathing photographer in infrared darkness
who fixes it with salts and chemistry
on prepared pulp of tree-scat

I am not a song of the dew or a poem of the dew
written in minor chords or with great words
spoken in wild whispers or sung in voices
that ring with ritual and abandon

I am just a drop of dew that gathers before dawn
without meaning, other than that which you give me
when the sun slices the horizon
to burst through your bedroom window
and send a shadow-line sweeping
like a rising curtain across the glittering green meadow of lawn
as you close your eyelids against the glare
and stretch out your hand, open-palmed and welcoming.

This morning

This morning I discovered the satisfaction
old men derive from sweeping the sidewalk.
The rhythmic scratching, vaguely reminiscent of sex,
not entirely empty of sensuality, the sticky shuffle of feet.
Starting on the porch, moving furniture a few feet one way
to clear its shadow of dust and grit and fallen leaves, feathers,
then moving it back in place, restoring order.

There's little gained, since yesterday
and tomorrow's likely to be the same, if it doesn't rain.
But what's surprising is the delight I feel
in finding, finally, one certain thing that I can return to
again and again, and know that the gathering drift of dust
and grit, flecked feather and leaf crumb
will go on long after I'm able to move it from one place
to another, with the sun climbing the peak of the roof
and its shadowline sweeping clean the walkway behind me.

There is no grave. There really is no grave.

Ode to Frenchtown, or, Why I live here

In this river town where I've lived
For all of this century and much of the last
I want a stranger to ask
Why I live here, so in answering
I'll come to know the answer.

If it's because of the mist that silently sets its palm on the Delaware at dawn
Or the long late day shadows that slink along Third Street
To disappear among trees crowding the Alexandria ridge
Or the reflection of the full moon in an indigo sky that shimmers on moving water,
Then I'll say, "The weather," and be done with it.

But if it is because here is where I live
With men and women I love and our many children
I know I'll go on and on.

Lost herd of horses

To Gail Cross, captain of our high school cheerleading squad

When I was ten, I taped a cherry bomb to
my mother's 78 recording of Sarah Vaughn
singing "Black Coffee" and sailed it
over the back yard fence into the schoolyard sky.
Back came a needle thin shard of black plastic that
pierced Scooter William's right eye and
left him a squinting fifth-grade goof.
The blast disquieted the neighbors
sent Jackie Miller's shepherd
into frothing hysterics, sent her baby brother
into hysterics plain and simple and
sent my father into action,
stripping the belt from around his waist.
"Jack," my mother called, "Don't kill him."

At twelve there was the silver-papered ashcan
that sizzled as Angelo LoBianco and I
passed it back and forth, white-eyed and frantic,
that took his ring and pinkie fingers and
forced him to learn to throw a football lefty
which, in ninth grade, he tossed 30 yards into the end zone
to take the last game against rival Redwood.

Then there was the M-80 that spread, when we
were sixteen, the beveled ribs of Egger Blaus'
galvanized trash can, lifting the lid
with smoke and stinking garbage and
thunder that thudded our chests,
left our ears ringing for an hour and

the hiss of water sloshing inside our
heads for days and days.

Then one late spring day in senior calculus
with lilacs blooming outside the bank of louvered windows
you swept behind the ear nearest me
a twist of chocolate hair, so heavy
with sunlight that it made me ache.
You shifted in the pocket of your one-piece desk
and crossed your mostly bare thighs so that
the long muscles there hollowed in a curving line.
You pressed your lips together and studied me
with dark eyes and the shadow at your cheek
resolved into an unrecognizable arc that
left me confused, a lit fuse,
trembling with desire.

I hated him

I hated him and that little snit puppet Clowny
whose annoying voice I knew was his anyway
with his pointed hat and painted head and stupid painted grin
or was that Kukla?

I don't remember a thing about it actually.
Probably there were cartoons and why was I watching, anyway?
Because I'd been planted there earlier
at the beginning or before, perhaps hours before.

"O, that Zenith TV raised you," said my cousin Ellen
forty-five years later, laughing at her memories of my childhood,
calling to acknowledge my birthday and to tell me
her latest boyfriend had cancer.
"She'd put you in the playpen in front of that little screen
and come back from time to time to see if you'd fallen asleep," Ellen
    said.
Perhaps got my head stuck between the reed brown bars
of my prison trying to touch the screen
or trying to turn it off in desperation, I wonder.

She is between the big mahogany console and me
her housedress soft and silky with flowers as big as my fists
flowers more vibrant than flowers
the cloth soft and bouncy not puffed out and stiff
like the gray dress Miss Frances wears on Romper Room
where the children sit in tight little circles
happily clapping their hands, fingers pointing in all directions at
    once
or if one began looking lost and suddenly frightened
tears welling in his eyes searching past the camera for his mother

instantly he is gone and replaced by another smiling child.
In the flash of her white flowered dress before me
blocking the lattice diamonds of wood over cloth-covered speakers
her swishing legs muffle the sound of Hopalong Cassidy's white horse Topper
thundering along a trail studded with boulders
less real than Miss Frances' gray dress.

She is handing me a glass of tepid apple juice at arm's length
as though she knows I am by now, mid-day, too dazed to hold it properly
fears a splash on her new open-toe shoes or
on the few polished toes that wiggle there
like tiny faceless creatures wearing red helmets
wriggling out from under the white leather
in an attempt to escape down the hall.
Then the real clown Clarabel lurches onto the scene
clutching a siphon seltzer bottle
squeezing the red bulb of a bicycle horn
racing round and round like a mad lost soul
panicked, intent, directionless, wild
chasing phantoms and children
who squeal and raise skinny arms to protect themselves
from buckets of water that become fluttering bits of bright confetti
and talk to that tiny sad cowboy with the frozen grin
clattering jaw strange dead legs and tiny stiff boots
a crippled rodeoman desperate for a wheelchair.

There was Darlene! And Bobby!
and the fat bald guy who hung around with Jimmy!
and Mickey Mouse and sputtering Donald and the others.
Who was Bozo? Who was that strange Indian?
What kind of creature was Goofy, anyway?
And why Kangaroo? Mr. Greenjeans, fine, but Kangaroo?
And the Merry Mailman, what was his name? Ray Something.
Dum... dum... the merry mailman, dum... dum... de dum dum dum

And something with three unnatural characters
three somethings I don't remember what but
I'd be let out of the playpen to watch them
she'd smooth a clear vinyl sheet over the TV screen to protect it
and I'd mark up the images with greasy crayons
in my random, colorblind way
while she swept from the playpen cookie crumbs
and fragments of uneaten grilled cheese, dried bits of burger
soft, oozing sections of tangerine and empty bags and boxes of breakfast cereal
and I'd watch her openly, distracted
watch the tug of flowers across her shoulders and hips
watch her stretch to wipe with a yellow sponge
spilt milk and juice and Jell-o and ice cream
hearing that soft scraping sound of cellulose on the thin plastic of the playpen mattress
leaving the slick cover damp and crinkly under my fat knees
when I'd be set back inside after my time on that little seat
with the picture of yellow ducklings and tiny white baby chicks
snapped in place in the pink-tiled bathroom
where she'd impatiently tap her painted nails on the porcelain sink
study herself in the mirror, arching first one than the other plucked brow
touching saliva with the tip of her tongue to gloss her upper lip
purse her lips, suck in her cheeks
gently scratching one perfect nostril with one perfect fingernail
then smiling at herself then frowning
picking a tiny fleck of lipstick from a perfect front tooth.

I'm watching Modern Farmer at 5 a.m.
dairymen sterilize a mechanical milker
then watching and watching Sunrise Semester
squinting at factories and machines or charts sagging with numbers
or men wearing ties saying loud incomprehensible words over and over
morning after morning sometimes learning to draw afternoons

from Jon Nagy whose beatnik beard seems somehow less real than
    Clowny's nose
but she'd quickly change the channel then because
I'd watch with my mouth open, spittle pooling on my shirt
as winter forests or fall meadows or distant snowy mountains
crawled from under his fingernails to fill the blank paper
shading here and there with the side of his thumb
showing how the light from the invisible sun always falls in the same
    direction
freezing the effect of an unseen breeze on crowded hemlocks
on smoke curling from a cheerful farmhouse under a threatening
cumulous that billows mysteriously at the slicing edge of paper.

But never people in the foreground or in the background
never people anywhere but on television anyway
or hurrying unseen down the corridor clattering noisily
along the tiny hexagonal black and ivory tiles
or out of sight at the dark apartment door at the end of the
    shadowed hallway
with surveys or samples or other times absent altogether
when I somehow knew she was speaking to little people who lived
    inside the telephone
distant, buzzing, always impatient until finally I hear her say
"Thank God it's over."

Then she'd be beside the playpen again
snap on the light from the floor lamp next to the television
where it was once again Ringmaster Claude Kirschner
with that stupid little puppet clown and he'd say:
"And now it's time for most of you to go to bed,"
and she'd hoist me in her arms and hold me close for the first time
    that day
and I'd smell in her hair Aquanet hairspray from the red-netted can
    in the bathroom
on her lips I'd smell smoke from a pack-a-day habit of Herbert
    Tareyton cigarettes

the sweet chemical aroma of makeup when my cheek pressed
    against hers
with my one hand spread on her opposite cheek my thumb in my
    own mouth
the scent of Vitabath lotion or Calgon bathwater beads coming from
    her in waves
as she rubbed the milk mustache from under my nose
lay me down into a crib I was already too big to sleep in
wearing laundered pajamas printed with holsters and horseshoes
    and spurs
elastic gripping my ankles and wrists like shackles.
She is brushing the hair from my damp forehead
with painted fingernails
planting a token kiss there, too
then wiping away the lipstick mark and... she is gone,
leaving the door open a crack
so the dark can leak out
little by little throughout the night
until enough of it has escaped
for daylight to squeeze in through the window
bringing with it the yeasty perfume of crusty rolls
and seeded rye and onion-and-poppyseed bialys
rising from Mittelman's Bakery six stories below
crawling up the walls of red brick and brown mortar
and wafting inside to tickle my nose and wet my mouth
and wake me wake me wake me to the sound of her footsteps
and the singing hinges of the bedroom door swinging open to
    morning.

From the kitchen comes the familiar hiss and babble of coffee
percolating in that dented aluminum coffee pot with its Bakelite
    handle
and across from my bedroom the collapsing white noise of the
    Zenith
becomes a man's voice announcing broadcast codes
and once again it is time for the combine and tractor and harvesters
and chickens and cows and horses and sheep and wheat and corn

and grim-faced men in broken shoes and sad-faced women in faded aprons

and barefoot children wearing too large or too small blue workshirts

and machines will break and rain will bruise fruit and fires will raze homes

and tornadoes will tear apart barns and livestock will breach fences and droughts

and floods and bankers and thieves and trucks and belching coal engines

and silos filled with maggots and rats and buzzing

and water turned into blood and biting insects and wild beasts

and boils and fiery hail and locusts and darkness and the death of the first born

and she stands me on the printed vinyl

to the rising music of Modern Farmer

and I take hold of the bars and watch

and watch and wait my turn.

Lost herd of horses

They are down there, in the mucky trash
among gum wrappers, and broken pencils, peach pits, twisted rigid orange rinds
a brass belt buckle and a lady's left silver shoe, scuffed and broken-strapped, the heel gone
dozens of crumpled cigarette packs, Marlboro boxes
blue and gold Chesterfields, bullseye Lucky Strikes
alongside cellophane and foil and shredded gray newsprint.

I can see them through the dull black bars of the grate set into the cement sidewalk
two lay together, one pitch black, the other white, her reins tangled in dark mane and tail
a paint pony is a half-step away, head buried beside a bottle of soda pop
a fourth and fifth, both white with manes and tails streaming, lie on their sides
their legs locked, as though fighting for leadership of this small herd of plastic horses
escaped somehow from my bedroom dresser, still in their fine rubber saddles and halters

Six floors up, down the checkerboard hallway of black and white hexagonal tiles
the barn door of the apartment swings wide, inside cigarette smoke clings to the curtains
the riders are gone, too: white-haired Hopalong Cassidy in his tight white shirt
Wild Bill Hickock in black vest and fringed chaps, his stiff pearl hat tumbled brim up
as though knocked from his head in a barroom brawl
one lone Tonto in hard plastic buckskin and two Lone Rangers in gunpowder blue

challenging each other, glaring behind their masks, neither will
   admit to being an imposter.
And horseless Roy Rodgers, painted blue eyes searching in the
   gloom for Bullet, for Dale,
for Trigger, who alone remains upstairs, patient, staring past the
   pasture of my dresser into the mirror.
My father won't ask, knowing I can't, at four-years-old, possibly
   know why
I have thrown this herd of horses into the catch basin in front of
   Mittleman's Bakery.
Six trips up and down, two feet per step, clutching the banister with
   one hand,

cradling the captured horses, cowboys and one Indian in the crook
   of the opposite arm.
I know they are ashamed to travel in such an undignified way
though I don't yet know there is a word for such feelings.
When, finally, my father has lassoed the last of them with kite string
   and
my mother has washed the filth from every leg and limb, I stare from
   bed at the crowded dresser corral,
ashamed, for Wild Bill, though he sits his horse well, will ride hatless
   through my childhood forever.

Many places

Many places that feel like home
are not home at all
and many places that do not feel like home
are home nonetheless.

This is your opinion at six-years-old
leaning coolly in 1956 against the front fender
of your father's 1949 black Plymouth
an open deck of playing cards held loosely in one small hand
ace of hearts, in black and white, visible at the bottom.

The steel of the car is hot against your backside
pressed blue slacks, pressed white shirt
the blue-and-white checked bowtie clipped to your collar
tickles your throat as you chew a stick of Juicy Fruit.

You wait with a tilted smile for a mother
to take your hand and walk with you six city blocks to school.
In the photograph on that first day of First Grade
your sailor's crew cut is shiny and stiff with wax.

The secret behind your grin is the wet-again lollypop
chosen at Frank's barber shop the day before.
You've hidden it in the pocket of your pants on the sly
and you don't yet know that it's become
studded with blue gray fuzz and bits of blond hair.

Roosevelt dime

As if I could re-ride the bicycle,
Sweep round the corner of the brick building
On Newark's long Bergen Street
And find myself flying again
Toward the open steel doors
Of the hardware store's delivery shoot.

See again the metal so close by
Its raised diamonds scuffed
With pedestrian shoe grease,
Tiny bits of trapped trash
Flecks of tobacco ash
The paper stem of a spent match
A rhinestone lost from a little girl's ring
The humped half of blackened peanut
The thick gob of a rabbi's cough
A Roosevelt dime, 1959, new, shining
Between rusted hinge and frame.

The dime.

I'd recall the dime lying weeks in bed
With my grandmother hovering and a fat black nurse
Whose body funk would wake me before she touched
My head to change the bandage.
I'd think of the dime instead of the sound of my father
Retching after watching her peel away the bandage the first time
And the edges of things were bright
But of the things themselves I could see nothing.

My father had slipped Hitler's grasp
To run headlong into America's crossed arms
Had worshipped Roosevelt on arrival
Though they grew apart as the spigot tightened
Ending the trickle of relatives.

Months later, as I sailed again and again in my blind daydreams
Toward the steel trap outside Epstein's Hardware
I'd see Roosevelt's silvery profile
Staring at the b in Liberty
Hair neatly parted and forever swept behind a shapely left ear
Jaw set and strong above In God We Trust
As though he himself was God
A cupped cheek that meant clenched teeth
Lips that one time might be smiling
But the next might be pressed in disapproval.

One morning, with the window open
And a woodpecker in the back yard knocking himself senseless
I woke and heard, "We have nothing to fear but fear,"
But Roosevelt had died years before and it was just the radio.
It was, I remember now, my tenth birthday.

Six poems about crows, by one who loves them

1
How glorious for the crow
despite its apparent mass
to weigh so little it would take
the feathers of 50 to make a pound.

No wonder, seeing one land so lightly
on an uppermost branch to survey
the terrain and complain, we insist,
despite all we're told, that a pound of gray lead
would fall faster than a black pound of feathers.

2
Crows, we're told, have no
bitter memories of loss, unlike
a robin or whippoorwill, which are known
to have had better days. Not like a
lark or nightingale, or canary,
lost in reverie,
trilling near lyrical song.

O, if you were a crow, you couldn't feel
smug or privileged, you couldn't look
down your black beak on even a peacock whose
song, like that of a guinea hen, is
no less jarring than yours, and equally ill-regarded.

3
I fell in love with crows twice. The first was when a black crowd of
    them
descended in their thermal-falling way into the acre of
trees that ring Vincent's Pond. I learned that
not all things that fall from great heights are doomed. I was
six, and couldn't stop staring at those great bodies
ebony and gleaming, hunching my shoulders at their grating call.

Then came the day I saw one — as close to me
as you are now, and as enormous — land beside
my father, asleep under the hot sun with a green towel on his head,
and snatch his wedding band from its rest
on the aluminum arm of the beach chair.
Without shrugging its wings beneath its hunched shoulders
or disturbing the old man's sleep, the black bird beat against the
    invisible
in a slow rise that seemed impossible or at least magical.
It didn't fly off so much as swing with lazy nonchalance
along invisible scrim to disappear into nearby crowded woods
and that day I knew why we love best our darkest clowns.

4
In my ears the rousing cries of crows were
those of skinny boys I knew from the little league field
who wore tightly cuffed split-knee jeans
and cheered at the annual summer rodeo, favoring riders who
were thrown from the Brahman too soon, and cheered again,
as the bruised cowboy drunkenly sauntered through rodeo ash
and dust with his back to the snot-flinging bull while the clown tried
to distract the beast — and us — crowing and flapping his arms.

5
She was tall and narrow at 13,
awkward and pimply, unlovely
and unloved or even welcomed

when she nursed then made a pet
of an orphaned baby crow. As a chick
it clung under her coat to her collar,
resting its coal black beak on her school sweater
and when it could fly it followed her from above
to land lightly on her shoulder and squawk
at children who mocked her and fly at them
to peck at their heads and
and pluck jewelry from their ears.

I met her years later, when she had become a beauty
and men would ask friends about the chick with the bird
and the crow would cock its head to one side
to see whether they had been among her earlier tormenters.
Her hair is no longer as black as its wings
and the music of her voice has become a breathy drawl
and the crow, she claims, will soon be 50.

6
When I say I've always been a fan of crows
I chiefly mean my entire adult life.

My mother told me I'd been frightened
of them as a child, that I thought she,
in that magical way of mothers, had
conscripted a murder of crows to spy on me
when out of her sight. So of course, I saw
or heard them everywhere I looked, or listened
and knew they were there to scold me
when I drifted, or even thought to.

Still, I grew to love them.

Unlike pretty birds, a crow is not prone
to preen in public. Its strut is one of

confidence, not pride — the crow knows its
reputation is, shall we say, not stellar, knows
its place, so to speak, and knows its vocalization,
that slow rasp of file on metal,
is not called song by any thinking person.

But that's just it, isn't it?
The crow's irritating voice,
the disharmony of its warning from a high wire
may as well be my father's stern nagging to pay attention,
pay attention, pay attention, fool. Life is short.

Deli Man

They say write what you know.
Well, I know delicatessen
I know pastrami
    the mad salt peppercorn molasses meat,
    soft and hot in your mouth
    mustard, tangy and sweet
    rye the crusty cousin to whiskey
I know slaw, too, wet and dreamy, crunchy,
    ground to bits by your molars
    and still an hour later wedged between the teeth
And pickles, those alchemists' cucumbers, I know them.

We cook a ton of corned beef a week
    boiled down from the size of Volkswagens to ten pound slabs
    we pull 'em from the kettle and slap 'em on the butcher block
    we cut the wedge of white fat from the pocket
    the greasy mother of flavor,
    the grandmother of all great food.
We stab the big thing with a wood-handled meat fork and
    heave it on the slicer, steaming against the circular knife
    that whirls as invisible as a lumberman's saw
    razor sharp, it hews a perfect slice
    and bits of moisture burst from the grainy fat of the deckle
    like tears to charm desire.
God, I know corned beef!

(I know shrimp salad, too, but not for publication)

Give me tongue, Herman
    rich, center cut tongue
    from the back of her schlongy cud to mine

    piled with glistening white potato salad
    studded with carrots, green peppers, diamond red onions
Give me a knish, dammit, brown and flakey
    with potato so soft it flows upon the fork
And lather it with mustard
    not Guilden's and not French's, God forbid!
    You know the one
    it doesn't have a brand name, man
    but it lives in the same neighborhood, same street
    on the same damn block, even, as Dr. Brown's Celray soda.

I don't even want to *talk* about chopped liver.

Starlings

I
I am nine or ten years old
walking to my grandfather's house on Conforti Avenue
passing the football field where older boys in shoulder pads
stretch to touch their toes
when a great turbulent noise rises
and a pitch of starlings clots in shifting knots
the bleached September sky.

Many-winged, they drop like falling black water
into a stand of oak and elm and maple
and all but disappear behind the leafy green glaze.

It swallows them whole, that tiny wooded lot,
a short wide block,
the buttonhole of a cloak of streets
lined with mean porchless houses needing paint.

I am transfixed, at nine or ten years old
as the starlings' chattering, rattles and whirrs and whistles
becomes a vast whirlpool of noise that drags into itself every other
    sound.

Then the sun tumbles end over end between goal posts
bounces wildly, leaving a gilt gash across the glassy surface of
    Vincent's Pond
as it slips behind the boathouse.

Settling into its own speckle-feathered dusk,
the wood is swollen with unseen starlings
thousands, tens of thousands, perhaps a hundred thousand
growing quiet then still.

It is dark.
The footballers are gone.
The moon not yet come.
There is no sign of the starlings, no sound.
it is still, just still, completely still.

II
Time came when I was the older boy in shoulder pads
trying to touch the toes of my cleats.
Then a man driving to work,
a steady man, marrying,
burying my grandmother,
burying my mother.

And I forgot entirely about birds falling through the sky like black water
until the morning of the day my son is born,
when a sudden spring breeze in the yard shakes free apple blossoms
that shower down and turn white the grass
in a great circle around my grandfather sitting in his wheelchair smoking a cigar.

Then from the apple came peeping of hatchlings
and the memory of starlings falling through the sky shouldered in
as a single robin dropped to the lawn
cocking his black-hooded head
pinning me with a long look from his black black eye
and that same moment my wife called from the kitchen, "It's time."

Of love

What happened at dinner, and after

We ate.
Baby lettuce, toasted pecans,
funky perfumed goat cheese
with its history of grass and sunshine.

We ate.
Black-flecked wild mushroom bisque
tasting of earthy beginnings in the lee of hundred-year hemlocks,
at the dark mouths of caves, beside slow-moving water.

We ate.
Angel hair pancake... corn, scallion and red pepper chutney,
regrets of summer and spring forgotten
as fall fell across Cape May like a glass bead curtain.

We touched glasses and ate.
Oysters, roasted in their Pleistocene shells, the glistening pouch of meat
a lover's tongue slipped between our lips,
yielding, releasing its sea salt syrup.

We ate.
Fruit, pastry, something of chocolate,
things that made us look into one another's eyes
and carry our shoes along the sand
with the full moon a silver disc in black heaven behind us.
Before us the sea rising and falling, thundering in the dark,
hissing about our feet in white foam ribbons.

You tilted your head beneath my chin like a violin,
the spinning air wove gossamer around us
and we rose, turning slowly, toward the silver disc in the black sky.
Your lips touched mine, earth became a distant echo
and we were gone.

Of love

We are mapping the territories, you know, of love.
An expedition. My Lewis to your Clark.

In you, I imagine Ptolemy in Alexandria,
peering into the night sky.
And me, a naïve scientist thrumming wire,
gathering rising notions,
thinking things through.

Then your reaching fingers
are at the pulse at my throat,
their tips touch my lips,
enter my mouth, exploring.
I bend my tongue to your liquid skin,
discover salt — and my eyes fill with
moonlight trembling on moving water.

Later, when the moon sets,
and we embrace in unremarkable darkness,
the concept of time remains in awkward disarray
and language, always somewhat inadequate,
always frail, is simply defeated.

A faucet drips in another room.
Somewhere downstream
an engine fails to start.

But here, now, with us,
things work the way tides do,
the way gravity works.
Agile electrons fly about

holding everything still.
Magnetic fields align in ordinary gentleness
and in every mountain pass
and at each river portage
heat rises.

What is there to talk about? (after reading Rilke on Rodin)

What is there to talk about, really?
Trials, noisy hope, the disappointments of age?
Unexpected joy, the pleasures of the kitchen
The pleasures of the bedroom, days or nights of pain?

Instead, sit with me shoulder to shoulder
Or cheek to cheek, or barefoot, lying down, holding hands
An hour will pass in thrumming silence, a day
Fix your gaze on me or far along the horizon

If we were to speak, would we speak of our children?
Would we speak of days past or those to come?
Perhaps we would speak of things we hold dear or of desperate
    longing
Certainly, of possessing or lacking money, or of things equally
    unimportant

Instead, let me watch you at your work, I like that best of all.
Hands shaping things, eyes measuring size and distance, leaning in,
Bending at the waist or stepping to one side to regard your work
    from a distance
If you hum or sing to yourself, so much the better.

What can be said will be said again and again.
Today, I would rather hear the soft scrape of your footstep
And see, as you turn toward me, how your hair rests just so on the
    collar of your coat.

We fall asleep loving and wake together laughing

You say,
come to bed,
or I do.
No matter.

Our bed is a farmer's field of
miracles in four seasons.
Our bed is the wide expanse of seas without end
rolling endlessly outward from everywhere.
Our bed is milk froth, jump rope, handwork,
the expanding universe, a slowly whirling
world of blue and green seen from a distance
through a white blanket of clouds.

The time we come
to bed is unimportant.
Neither is time
when we are here.

At night, our bed is our home, a snapped sheet
over a soft cushion of warm air.
At night, our bed is the Alamo, an archeological site
a hewn block tumbled from the Sphinx at Giza.
At night, our bed is a volcano, the I Ching,
saffron-scented smoke curling from the Oracle at Delphi,
a sacrificial alter sticky with the blood of ancestors
who sing and grumble all night long,
the strings of a violin, the strings of a harp, a lute,
the single string of a diddley bow.

George Washington slept here,
and Columbus the night before sighting land,
Devi, Delilah, Catherine the Great,
Rumi the Sufi, Don Juan the mystic,
Clarabelle, Houdini, Smokey the Bear.
In our bed, David composed poems to God
Between bouts loving Bathsheba.

By day our bed is buried treasure unearthed,
secrets revealed, the vault of Alexander the Great unsealed,
the Sixth Book of Moses concealed beneath eons of dust
at the back of a hidden cave near Hebron
where our father Abraham is buried.
The sheet drawn taut across our bed is the patriarch's shroud,
Mohamed's shawl, Gandhi's longhi.
By day our bed is a secret panel, a passage to India,
a shimmering portal, the night sky in 1609 when
Henry Hudson nosed the Half-Moon through the narrows.

In our bed at night, we fall asleep loving and wake together
    laughing.
We sleep soundly when we sleep,
our limbs twisted into unsustainable knots,
the rocking rhythm of the universe is our pillow,
a bobbing channel buoy marking safe waters.

In our bed at night and daytime
we make love loudly when we make love loudly,
loud enough to wake neighbors if we had neighbors.
When we make love quietly, love-making is a meditation on making
    love.

Every morning in our bed as dawn drifts in
you share the history if your intricate dreams
tracing each through its own complex mathematics

as mist rises from the river
to leave its trace across our bed like the snail of time
spreading diamonds that are set ablaze by sunlight
day after day after day.

From the earth to the moon, and back

Moonlight on the river
lifts you, an arm beneath
your back arching against the
strength of gravity, the grasping
weight of the water, glistening
skin sliding over sinew, your
breath a sibilant shadow shaking
the leaves of trees along the bank,
the coming flood tugging at the
roots, at the flesh. Your lips,
eyelids wet and fluttering
before the rising wind, your
belly and thighs trembling.

Then, when we wake
from loving, arms and legs
inspired liquid, mouths
so many mouths, moving
fingertips at still-hungry lips,
the mist presses down, lifts us
and sets us lightly upon the earth
alert, measuring, weighing.

Then again comes the fading clang of
a bell echoing in a vacuum,
a surging rainbow of
blood and green river grass
rooted in golden water
and with that, the sun

rises to dissolve the last
distance between us
and we feel everything
finally released, tumble.

James Beard was a great bedtime reader of cookbooks

These he read, he said, for gastronomic dreams
of rhubarb and fiddleheads in spring, of pumpkin and sole in fall.
I read your mad letters at midnight for the whitewater dreams of
    near death they induce
of calling and falling among grasping limbs, of longing and of
    unutterable desire.

On mornings like these, I like to find your letters crumpled and
    damp,
clutched under a pillow or between your breasts
the sheets of paper soft as shed skin.
I like to see the ink stains on your thighs and remember how,
when your children were babies,
milk would seep from your nipples after sex.
Or I might suddenly recall how, sitting in the smoke-fragrant
    moonlight that first fall,
we settled forever what we would or would not eat while naked in
    bed.

I like to think, then, of tomorrow or the night before or any time at
    all when we were happy.
Later, I will find something you've left behind, like your hair brush,
    or your travel clock
or your wedding band, or a cold and abandoned cup of tea,
and see the fragment of pigment where your lips touched the lip of
    my cup.

Shadow in the dark

Earlier tonight I saw a woman with hair like yours
as sleekly brown as a holiday chestnut
shining like rainfall at the nape of her neck, with dark shadows
falling through it the way shadows fall through yours.

She listened to music stands and chairs moving behind the curtain
with her head tilted to the left, as you would have listened
shoulders squared, wrists flat to the worn wooden arms
of the school auditorium seat, her back flat in its curving pocket.

She'd come early — as you would have done
and chose a seat a few rows from the front and to one side
quietly watching the curtain ripple with obscure traffic
her shoulders seemed to rise and fall with my breath
as siblings, parents, grandparents crowded in.

No one joined her, though once she waved to someone I could not see
and the seats to her left and right stayed empty
when the lights dimmed and the curtain rose and the first class filed out
to fill the risers and search for their mothers, blinking against the lights,
and I saw once or twice a small motion of her hand as a shadow in the dark.

The children came and went,
my older with his trumpet, the younger her clarinet
the younger again with the chorus.
When the principal spoke, lights came up and
I looked again for the woman who looked like you from the back

100

but she had turned or leaned forward — and, with the familiarity
    gone
I lost her.

Through the night, snow fell in silence so deep that I
woke before dawn forgetting that I was alone and
felt your steady breath against my neck and
saw the fingertips of your hand moving like a shadow in the dark
to settle the blanket over my shoulder and
heard a whisper that was not a whisper
but only silence stirring the curtain of memory.

Sunrise

Determined, with three vacation days left,
I head for the beach to see the sun rise.
Above, a brilliant moon in an indigo sky.
To the south, lightning flashes
behind a bulge of banked clouds.

Climbing the wooden walk and slatted stairs
through manmade dunes, I hear the surf
collapsing heavily with reliable and regular pomp.
Closer now, the sound of the thing grows articulate and granular
and I hear the unseen surf in all its surfness,
its muttering swell, the crackling crack of waves
rising, losing their integrity and breaking apart,
the long slow thud as each hangs as thick as a hedge
then rolls upon itself along a long low angle,
hissing across the sand as it spreads in wide white tongues
leaving its trace of no trace over and over for eternity.

I stop.

The moonlight gives way to the lightening sky, but no visible sunrise.
A bird I can't see repeats a melody I don't recognize
and, still unseen, the churning flood rings and runs, rings and runs,
until I turn and rethread my way, tasting salt in the air with each
    breath,
each sand-grinding step worrying the rain-spongy boards.

Meanwhile, you sleep on, your lips
parting and closing in a rhythm

as familiar to me as my own.

Across your chest, your right arm
rises and falls. Then butter-and-yolk
light oozes over the windowsill
and you wake to my morning
and we make love in our languid
rolling way, dancing, hearing
at a distance and near at hand
the known and unknown
music of the universe.

At last, the gift

A day passes I don't think of her.
Her black hair, cordovan skin, eyes bright as tar,
laughter, rising and falling like familiar music,
her touch as light as sunlight, her scent no heavier than dew.

We argued and she was gone without saying goodbye.
I nailed shut the fallboard of her piano,
burned her Bach and Shubert and wore bare the stair treads
searching for photos I hadn't felt a need to take.

Later, her laughter recalled would catch me up
as would memory of her eyes shining behind G-clef curls,
or her bare skin polished by rainfall or the cruel diminuendo of her
    fragrance
fading from bedsheets until I was stripped of desire to sleep on
    them.

That was decades ago
and no one I know now knows her name to say aloud.

But driving last night,
invisible behind the wheel,
I was joined at a stoplight by a woman who,
had time stopped forty years, might have been her.

As I waited, staring and breathless,
she regarding in the mirror her dark eyes and G-clef curls.
She touched the pillow of her lip with the tip of her tongue.
Then red became green, and
at last, she left me the gift of watching her drive away.

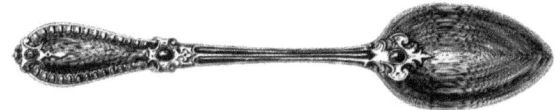

About the Author

Warren Cooper is a public relations strategist specializing in crisis communications, reputation management and litigation support. His poems have appeared in *U.S. 1 Worksheets*, the *New Brunswick News Tribune*, and *Ode to Hunterdon*. In no particular order, he's owned restaurants, been an investigative reporter and a New Jersey mayor, taught journalism and film at Raritan Valley Community College and psychology at Rutgers, where he earned a doctorate in the field.

About the Publisher

BLAST PRESS

"A book should be a ball of light in your hands."
— Ezra Pound

This past year, **BLAST PRESS** expanded its publishing program in several new directions. We have our first anthology—which is distinct from a magazine—with representative New Jersey poets with our *Palisades, Parkways & Pinelands,* a generous almost 300 page collection of over 30 poets. Another direction is the illustrated collaboration between H. A. Maxson and Dorothy Wordsworth in a new kind of "found poetry" that is a beautiful mash-up of a living poet and his long-dead collaborator's nature notebooks. *The Changing Room* is another first for BLAST PRESS, a fully-illustrated long poem by Carrie Hudak that blends dream and reality as a child's story might, but with adult themes of death and a sophistication of tone unusual in an illustrated tale. *Surfing for Jesus* is a lively new work by Susanna Rich, exploring religious themes and impacts of growing up in a church tradition in late-twentieth-century America. Joe Weil and Emily Vogel's "responsorials," are an ongoing dialog with poem answering poem in their unusual and emotionally intimate *West of Home.* Last year, **BLAST PRESS** released the widely published author Emanuel di Pasquale's *Knowing the Moment,* a delicate paean to his life on the Jersey Shore. And **BLAST PRESS** continues its primary tradition of supporting uncollected poets with a first-time poetry book by Mathew V. Spano, *Hellgrammite*. I would like to extend a special thank you to our authors and editors, and to our enthusiastic readers, for all you do to enliven the world of poetry.

With best regards,

Gregg Glory
(Gregg G. Brown)
Publisher

Meet Me in Botswana: What is BLAST PRESS?

A speech for national poetry month about BLAST PRESS

Ab li dolen in l'air
[look up: beauty falls from the air]

As we all know, April is "International Guitar Month." But my heart twangs for poetry, and I was invited here to tell you a little bit about a tiny poetry publishing company called **BLAST PRESS**.

Let's start with what **BLAST PRESS** is not. **BLAST PRESS** is not a community. It is not a community-building venture. It is not by, about, or for "the people." Unlike the pretentious anthologies that weigh down university shelves and slander the individual by gluing him into some historian's scripted story, **BLAST PRESS** is not a collection of individual voices expressing the vibrancy, meaning, and tradition of the creative community—nor of any community. In this respect, **BLAST PRESS**, as its critics have bitterly asserted, is nothing at all.

BLAST PRESS has published over 100 chapbooks and softbacks by some thirty authors over the past quarter century. Each author's work stands singularly alone and apart. **BLAST PRESS** does not take part in the mish-mosh of the magazine market, where a hundred tentative voices are corralled by brute binding into an ersatz herd. We go alone, each of us, to where the crocs swim alertly in the bulrushes and the nights are long. Meet me in Botswana, if you will meet with me at all.

What is a chapbook? A chapbook is a saddle-stapled booklet of plain paper stock folded in half with a sheet of colored card stock for a cover. In the first decade, booklets would be stapled together by hand, each staple closed with a bloody fingertip to save the two-cent per staple cost. All small publishers are unified in this regard: we are exceedingly cheap.

In the next few minutes, for a brief moment, we will hear the voices of some poets that have been published by **BLAST PRESS**. Their words have been put into chapbooks with a **BLAST PRESS** logo on the back, and my current address somewhere inside the front flap. Words torn from the air and swatted into print. That is all. But, that is everything.

Author Ethos

BLAST PRESS is what I would call a "micro-publisher." We usually publish poetry book under 150 pages in length. Our print runs are usually under 150 copies per edition. And **BLAST PRESS** has published over 150 books and chapbooks from some 25 authors in its career. The entire cost is assumed by **BLAST PRESS**, so we are the publisher, and not a vanity press or service.

    BLAST PRESS has been sustaining its small operation—in the black, mind you, no small feat—for about 25 years now. We have had a few more ambitious titles where the book itself, the author, and **BLAST PRESS** decide to dedicate the extra resources needed to make the event a success.

    Part of the **BLAST PRESS** ethos is to keep the authors in charge of their work so that they can maintain maximum control of their creative material in the out-lying years and don't need to be writing to **BLAST PRESS** for permission to re-publish snippets or poems.

BLAST PRESS catalog available at:
amazon.com/author/gregglory
and gregglory.com

    Our Credo
Do not dispraise the light
That, singing whatever's brightest,
Undoes the theft of night—
—Touch to caress, or move to love,
As this thoughtless rhyme does prove.
From **Ascent**

A Solitary Headstone
Niggling addendum to "Meet me in Botswana"

Magazines, published with a week's, month's, quarter's or even a year's date grow elderly on the shelves in a way that a collection of one individual's work never can. What year does Shakespeare's book expire? Horace is renewed year by year, no matter how worn his saws may wane. But a magazine or casual collection of miscellaneous artifacts, no matter how august the individual members of the find, retain an interest for us mostly as a time capsule. Even the Egyptian tombs of the pharaohs hold more interest for us because of what they reveal about the era of their creation than for what they say about their putative occupants. Old poetry quarterlies are no different, although they may contain an Endymion.

This is why **BLAST PRESS** is dedicated to publishing single-author volumes and stand-alone essay collections almost exclusively. Unless a poet is unknown, there is no point in his publication being undertaken by a small press. And if an author is unknown, he is best presented to an unacquainted public in his own exclusive company. It is always wisest to let a guest unroll at least a few of his favorite tales before we escort him from the house. What is characteristic and worthwhile in the poet's voice will quietly assert itself over the course of his varied pieces much better than if we merely heard his alba or evensong in isolation, let alone in the cacophonous squawk of a miscellany. To the marriage of true minds, ours and the author's, let not serial publication admit impediments. Only appearing in magazines and periodicals is like never having a final resting place—a poet without a plot.

BLAST PRESS
324B Matawan Avenue
Cliffwood, NJ 07721
(732) 970-8409
gregglory.com

Also Available

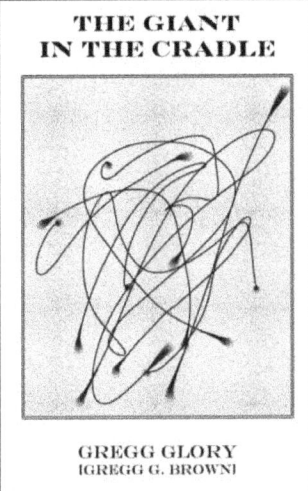

The Giant in the Cradle
Gregg Glory
[Gregg G. Brown]

List Price: $4.50
5.06" x 7.81"
Black & White on Cream
136 pages
ISBN-13: 978-1492396055
ISBN-10: 1492396052
BISAC: Poetry / American

FROM THE POEM "HEIGHT OF SUMMER"

Here is the day, the bridal day undaunted;
Here noon, at highest noon... hesitates...
The height of summer, at its crest arrested,
Held between warm hands to kiss—
The levitated real at pause in sun's perfection;
Paused because we cannot see, cannot imagine
Beyond such ripeness—

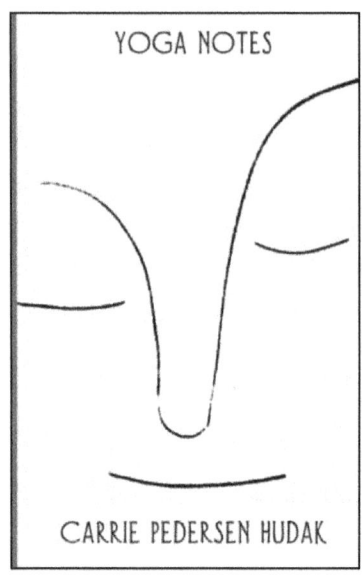

Yoga Notes
Carrie Pedersen Hudak

List Price: $4.50
5" x 8"
66 pages
ISBN-13: 978-1494330958
ISBN-10: 1494330954
BISAC: Body, Mind & Spirit

From the first essay: Just Practice

When I tell people I am a yoga teacher, they often say, I could never do yoga. I can't even touch my toes. Great, I say, you are already practicing awareness, that's part of the practice. Can you breathe? If you can breathe, then you can do yoga.

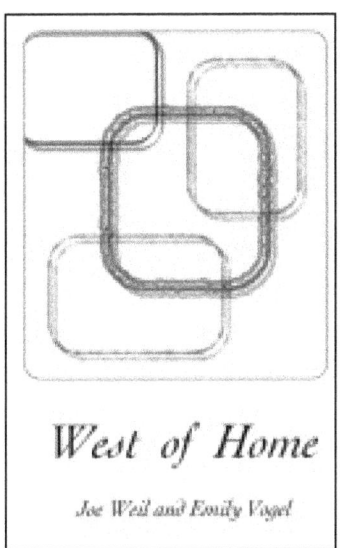

West of Home
Joe Weil, Emily Vogel

List Price: $10.00
Paperback: 98 pages
ISBN-10: 0615878415
ISBN-13:9780615878416
8 x 5 inches

From the Introduction

"West of Home" is a collaborative book of poetry which reflects the present and ongoing sentiments of Joe Weil and Emily Vogel. It includes 14 "responsorial" poems (call and response), between the two poets, as they respond to one another's themes and ideas, as well as two sections of poems, one for each poet's individual work.

Self-Symponies
Daniel Weeks

List Price: $10.00
Paperback: 146 pages
ISBN-10: 0692238581
ISBN-13: 978-0692238585
7.4 x 9.7 inches

From the Introduction

Inspired by listening to the four symphonies of Johannes Brahms, Daniel Weeks's Self-Symphonies explore the landscapes, cityscapes, and seascapes that are the backdrop to a life lived on the New Jersey shore. The four long poems in this collection provide meditations on family, inheritance, and loss, society, nature, and culture, and stasis and change—all of the elements that Coleridge said bething the individual self.

The Pilot Light
Gregg Glory
[Gregg G. Brown]

List Price: $5.50
Paperback: 132 pages
ISBN-13: 9781511941921
5.5 x 8.5 inches

About *The Pilot Light*

The poems in Gregg Glory's The Pilot Light are about relationships—with family, friends, and lovers—along with reminiscences of a childhood spent close to nature in the New Jersey countryside. Glory is particularly adept at exploring the significant and oftentimes intimate moments that define our most important relationships, moments which, in turn, help us create the story of the self.

Knowing the Moment
Emanuel di Pasquale

List Price: $12.95
Paperback: 131 pages
ISBN-13: 9781503117471
5.5 x 8.5 inches

About *Knowing the Moment*

    Emanuel di Pasquale has never been one to shy away from the more difficult aspects of living a full and engaged human life, and Knowing the Moment is perhaps his most searing work in this regard, as he confronts the hardships he encountered while growing up in his native Sicily. But these kinds of revelations are never the final word in his poetry. Tough times always seem to point him back to love—as he casts his mind back to life in Sicily or engages with the present in his poems about Long Branch, N.J.

The Hummingbird's Apprentice
 Gregg Glory
 [Gregg G. Brown]

List Price: $4.50
Paperback: 159 pages
ISBN-10: 1511941928
ISBN-13: 9781511941921
5.1 x 7.8 inches

From *The Hummingbird's Apprentice*

ROADSIDE WINE

Pull off 71 suddenly, onto
a wide shoulder of dust and grass.
weigh down a length
of brown barbwire fence
like a wave of honey breaking.
Excited, splash ankle-deep
into the unhurrying surf
full of velvety bee sounds, and select
one perfect blossom. It is
so sweet in the slow afternoon.
And, where you've cut your thumb,
a thrill of air catches.

American Songbook
Gregg Glory
[Gregg G. Brown]

List Price: $3.75
Paperback: 98 pages
ISBN-10: 1482703297
ISBN-13: 9780692238585
5.5 x 8.5 inches

The Old Truculence

A note concerning the basic arc of this book of poems—to re-register grace and freedom as America's primary metier.

Freedom breeds elegance. Not the inbred elegance of aristocracy, where beautiful ladies eventually come to resemble their Russian wolfhounds. Nor, simply, the truculent elegance of that sly Benjamin Franklin who, as ambassador to the French Court, refused to bow before King Louis the 16th or doff his coonskin cap.

Freedom breeds the desire to create one meaningful action with your entire life—the effortful elegance of the artist that James Joyce defined as the willingness to gamble your whole life on the wrong idea, a bad aesthetic, or, it may be, a genuine triumph. And America has created, and can still create, a unique scale of opportunity for such elegant "throws of the dice," as Mallarme might say. A natty Fred Astaire (originally Austerlitz), gliding with the ease of an ice skater as he backs Rita Hayworth (a gal from Brooklyn) into immortality to a tune penned by the Jewish Jerome Kern in an industry patented in the U.S.A. is but one example of the scale of that opportunity.

When you are free to do anything, a desire grows in the breast not to do just anything, but to do the best thing—and that is an aesthetic dilemma. The mere accumulation of capital, or the

arbitrary exercise by minor government regulators of petty power, are two classic examples of the desire for a meaningful expression of life-status that lack the aesthetic instinct. Such timid ambitions grow most strongly where the full range of light is narrowed, and the blossom of selfhood must twist around corners to open its ruby glory in a thinning patch of sunlight.
 Gregg Glory
March, 2013

Come, My Dreams
Come gather round me, multitudinous dreams
That in the dim twilight are murmuring soft;
Come lay by my head in the pillow-seam;
Come carry my freighted heart aloft.

O, I would dare dream as few men dream
Beyond the cruel cudgel of the strong,
Beyond the purpled tapestries of is and seems
Hung before my eyes, beyond cold right or wrong.

Also Available List

Anthologies
Palisades, Parkways & Pinelands
Jersey Shore Poets

Susanna Fry
30 Poems

James Dalton
Instead

Magdalena Alagna
The Cranky Bodhisattva

Rusty Cuffs
[Thad Rutkowski]
Sex-Fiend Monologues III

Sarah Avery
Persephone in Washington

George Holler
Erotic Logic

Jacko Monahan
One-Legged Poetry

Daniel J. Weeks
X Poems
Les Symbolistes
Self-Symphonies
Virginia

Carrie Pedersen Hudak
Yoga Notes
The Arms of Venus
Queens Arms
The Queen of Cakes
The Changing Room
Bee Loud Glade

Sharon Baller
Venus Has Gone Insane Again

Joe Weil
West of Home

Emily Vogel
West of Home

H. A. Maxson
Grasmere
Call It Sleep
A Commonplace Book

Emanuel Di Pasquale
Knowing the Moment
Poems in Sicily and America

Mathew V. Spano
Hellgrammite

Linda Johnston Muhlhausen
Elephant Mountain

Warren Cooper
What Happened at Dinner, and After

Gabor Barabas
Collected Poems

Lord Dermond
[Daniel B. Dermond]
13 Stories High
Ghosts and Princes Revised
Hourless Grail
Inner Dominion
Lords Miscellany
The Mortal Words
Sacred Blades
The Unaging Muse

John Dunfy
Spinning Wheels

Joie Ferentino
BELM

Chuck Moon
God-Speck Exhibitions

Brandi Mantha Grannett
Floaters

Mary Jane Tenerelli
'Til Death Do Us Part

Gregg Glory [Gregg G. Brown]
Adoring Thorns
The Alarmist
American Bacchanalia
American Descants
American Songbook

Antirime
Ascent
Assembling the Earth
Autobiographies
A/voi/d/ances
Benedict Arnold
Black Champagne
Brain Cell
Burning Byzantium
The Cabana at the Equator
Constellations in December
Chaos and Stars
Contemporaries
Dear Planet Jesus
The Death of Satan
A Deepening Sea
The Departed Friend
Deus Abscondis
Digital Boy
Disappearing Acts
Divine Revolt
Dr. Kilmer's Ocean-Weed Heart Remedy
Down By Swansea
Eating the Cliffside
Evil Interludes
The Falcon Waiting
Ghosts and Princes Revised
The Giant in the Cradle
Greetings from Mt. Olympus
Hell, Darling
The Hummingbird's Apprentice
Hurry Up, Hurricane!
Hymns
The Impossible Mesa
Interregnum Scribbles

It's the Sex Pistols!!!!
Jan and Marsha
The Life of Riley
The Maybe Plagues
Mercury Astronauts
A Million Shakespeares
Naked Eloquence
Nobody Poems
Night, Night
Of Flares, Of Flowers
On Being a Human Bean
The Pilot Light
Platinum Lips [CD]
Prometheus Bound
The Queen of Cakes
A Raven's Weight
Red Bank
Repetitions on the Rappahannock
Rose Lasso
Saving Cinderella
Shreads of Verity
Seven Heavens
The Singing Well
Sipping Beer in the Shadow of God
The Sleepy Partridge
The Soft Assault
Soul-Splitter
Spotty the Spot-tacular Cat
Supposing Roses
Supreme Day
The Sword Inside
The Timid Leaper
Torturous Splendours of the Dream
Ultra
Unimagined Things

Venus and Vesuvius
Vindictive Advice
A Volcano Island
Wild Onions
XXX Sonnets
Youth Youth Youth

www.ingramcontent.com/pod-product-compliance
Lightning Source LLC
Chambersburg PA
CBHW020940090426
42736CB00010B/1207